ON PREACHING

Donald Coggan

ON PREACHING

London
SPCK

First published 1978
SPCK
Holy Trinity Church
Marylebone Road
London NW1 4DU

The Bishop Martin Memorial Lectures 1975

Printed in Great Britain by
Hart-Talbot Printers Ltd., Saffron Walden, Essex

ISBN 0 281 03657 8

For Burgon Bickersteth
who loves Canada
its Church
and people
and who is loved by them
and by the author of these lectures

Contents

Preface

It was a great privilege to be allowed to give the Bishop Martin Memorial Lectures in May 1975 in the College of Emmanuel and St Chad, Saskatoon, Canada. More than thirty years previously, I had stayed in the house of Bishop and Mrs Martin when he was Bishop of Saskatchewan (1939-60). I recall vividly his upstanding figure, his infectious laugh, his hospitable home, his care for his clergy. It was a special joy to have his widow and daughters present at the College when I gave the lectures which had been endowed in his memory.

To the Bishop of Saskatoon and Mrs D. A. Ford whose generous hospitality my wife and I enjoyed during our stay in their city, and to the Principal and staff of the College who welcomed us so warmly, I pay my tribute of gratitude. Canada has had a place in our hearts since we first went to serve there in 1937. Later visits, and especially that of 1975, only serve to deepen our love for its Church and people.

DONALD CANTUAR:

Old Palace,
Canterbury.

Acknowledgements

Thanks are due to the following for permission to quote from copyright sources:

Hodder & Stoughton Ltd: *Convictions* by Donald Coggan

The Methodist Publishing House: *The Word and the Words* by Colin Morris. Published in the U.S.A. by the Abingdon Press.

Biblical quotations from the Revised Standard Version of the Bible, copyrighted 1946, 1952, © 1971, 1973, by the Division of Christian Education of the National Council of the Churches of Christ in the U.S.A., are used by permission.

1
Bifocal Anglicanism

A congregation of faithful men,
in the which the pure Word of God is preached,
and the Sacraments duly administered.

1 Bifocal Anglicanism

It was more than thirty years ago that, during the summer vacations, I took part in a number of schools of preaching in Western Canada and elsewhere. Those were the days—to mention but a few of the bishops then at work—of Archbishops Derwyn T. Owen and Ralph Sherman, of Bishops Hallam and Steer and Fleming ('Archibald The Arctic') and Sovereign and Renison and Beverley, good men and true, to whom the Canadian Church owes a great debt.

These schools of preaching forced me to do some hard thinking about preaching—its biblical and doctrinal basis, its theory and practice, and so on. On my return to England, Geoffrey Fisher, who was then Bishop of London and was to become Archbishop of Canterbury, asked me to lecture to his clergy. I took up and developed some of the material which I had used in Canada, and it appeared in 1945 under the title *The Ministry of the Word* (reprinted 1964). *Stewards of Grace* followed in 1958, and I have written and lectured on the subject, on and off, ever since.

In more recent years, in so far as I have had opportunity to write, I have found myself at work on other themes. But all the time, as college principal and as bishop and archbishop, I have been at the job of preaching, practising the art (if, as I think it can, it may be called an art), fulfilling the calling (as I think it can more adequately be described). In fact, for something close on half a century—for I tried to preach before I was ordained—I have been under the joyful tyranny of being a minister of the word.

I use the phrase 'joyful tyranny' advisedly. Preaching *is* a tyranny. I refer not only to the fact that Sunday comes round with an inexorable regularity and makes demands which must needs be met. I refer also to the fact that we know that we must not offer to the Lord a second-rate offering; only the best we can produce will do. I think of the demands which this makes on a man's freshness and devotion and reading and thinking and praying. A tyranny indeed! But a *joyful* tyranny—who would be without it who has been called and commissioned? I suppose a mother finds the care of her family in the early years demanding and tyrannical. But deprive her of her brood, and you have the epitome of bereavement and of misery.

When the invitation came to give these lectures, I was at first dubious about the wisdom of acceding to the suggestion that their subject should be preaching. Had I not said or written all that I had to give on this subject? I thought it over, and decided that there were still matters on my heart and mind related to preaching which I would like to share with you. Perhaps, in the mercy of God, since you and I share in this ministry, the passing on of some of my convictions might be of help to you. At least, these convictions have stood the test of the years, and have been tried out in a variety of circumstances and in many different parts of our Anglican Communion.

Let me begin with a story. Some years ago, in the course of my work as Archbishop of York, I went to a certain town in my Province. It had as its main glory an ancient and famous church. The incumbent, with commendable vigour, had raised a large sum of money to refashion the church and to restore it to something of its former glory and to adapt it for greater usefulness under modern conditions. I was to be present at its rehallowing at a great Eucharist, and was to preach. The greatest possible care had been put into the preparation of the service. Architecturally, the great feature was the altar,

4

central and resplendent. There could be no doubt that the Church of England was a sacramental Church, nor where it was that her children should kneel to be fed. The architect, the craftsmen, the silversmiths, all had given of their best. There was one focus. You could not miss it.

'This is very fine, Vicar. You have done magnificently. Now—you have asked me to preach. *Where do I preach from?*' 'They will bring you in a little stand, Archbishop, when the time comes.' And they did. A poor, paltry thing it was, liable to collapse if by chance I leaned upon it, the sort of temporary contraption from which any man might have scorned to give out the notices of the week. This was to be the thing from which the everlasting gospel was to be proclaimed. As soon as the sermon was over, it was taken away into oblivion. And good riddance, too!

The service over, I was introduced to the distinguished architect. I complimented him on so much that was good in the work that he had done. But while I was musing the fire had kindled. Then spake I with my tongue. 'When will you ecclesiastical architects', I said, 'give us *Anglican* ecclesiastical architecture? Is it not time that a visitor from some other tradition than ours should be able to see, by the very architecture of the building, that Anglicanism is "bifocal" in its means of grace, that the living God comes to us *both* in the sacrament of the Body and Blood of Christ *and* in the sacrament of the Word?' 'Yes', said the architect, in reply to my protest and distress. 'Yes, I see what you mean. I appreciate the point. I did in fact talk it over with the Vicar. But he said there was no need for a pulpit. He just speaks off the cuff.'

Three months later I went on holiday to Sweden. I

visited its churches. I could not read nor speak its language. What would the architecture of the churches tell me about its theology? This is what I found: great honour was obviously done to the sacrament of the Body and Blood of Christ. The altars of these churches were ornate and lavish in their accoutrements. Above them were figures—the Father in his almightiness, the Son in his passion, Moses with his commandments and Aaron with his censer, saints, apostles, martyrs in goodly array. There was no doubt about the importance of the Eucharist if we were to judge by what the architects and craftsmen had to say. And what about the sacrament of the Word? Here again was magnificence—a throne indeed! And immediately above the head of the preacher, suspended from the elaborate sounding-board, as often as not was the figure of the Dove, symbol of the Holy Spirit, eloquent of the fact that in the ministry of the Word, *God* is at work; this is no mere man prating.

I contrasted what I had seen in that town in my Province—and I noted that what I saw there was repeated in all too many English churches—with what I saw in Sweden. And I asked myself, if a complete stranger to English and to Swedish worship were to come, without further instruction, to see the churches of these two countries, what would he deduce as to their respective theologies of Word and Sacrament? I think the answer is clear; and I am distressed.

Do not let me be misunderstood. I am not, of course, suggesting that for an effective ministry of Word or Sacrament an elaborate setting is called for. That is not my point. All that is needed for the first is a man of God, a congregation, and the Bible. All that is needed for the second is a celebrant, a congregation, a bottle of wine and a loaf of bread. There may or may not be elaborations on that theme. What I am asking is whether, from the point of view of architecture, that particular instance of English arrangement or the Swedish balance of Word and Sacrament the better sets out the truth of the New Testament. I have no doubt about the answer.

My quarrel with that English church, and others like it, is that they are un-Anglican. If that is so, then I want our ecclesiastical architects to be told by our theologians and by our parish priest practitioners and by the parishioners throughout the Anglican Communion, that they must set forth in wood and stone and metal and other crafts that Anglican balance of Word and Sacrament which is explicit in our formularies and which derives from the New Testament. Listen to Article 19:

> The visible Church of Christ is a congregation of faithful men, in the which the pure Word of God is preached, and the Sacraments be duly ministered. . . .

Or re-read the services of the Ordinal, according to which you were made deacon and ordained priest, and you will find the same balance maintained. And if you come to be consecrated bishop in the Church of God, you will note that, at the most solemn moment of that most solemn service, the only thing which the Archbishop will put in your hands will be a copy of the Bible. There is no getting away from the centrality of the Word, if you listen to the emphasis of our formularies.

Perhaps you wonder why I am making such heavy weather of a point which to some may be self-evident. I do so, because I see in England at the present time a grave danger of an upsetting of that balance which I believe is crucial for the well-being of our people. Let me set out what is in my mind, and you must judge whether what I say is relevant to your situation in Canada during

7

the last quarter of this century.

In recent years there has been, in practically all sections of the Church of England, a new emphasis on the parish Eucharist as the main service of Sunday worship. 'The Lord's service on the Lord's day for the Lord's people.' So we seem to have been recovering the pattern of the first days of Christian worship. How joyful such services can be—with music, with the participation of young and old, male and female, in the leading of it, at any hour of morning or evening as fits the area or the occasion. This surely is right. By this we are being enriched. In this I for one rejoice. At the same time I find myself asking questions. In the general euphoria which is the result of our recovery of eucharistic worship, what has become of the ministry of the Word? We live in days when, generally speaking, it seems wise to limit the length of a service to an hour and little more. Supposing that there are many communicants and few administrants, several hymns and two or three lections, what is left for the preaching of the Word? All too often, the answer is, Very little—seven minutes, perhaps, or ten. Let it be said in passing that I think this is the result of bad liturgical management. I am not at the moment saying how I think things should be done. I am only pointing to what in fact does happen, and happen, I believe, very frequently indeed.

The clergyman finds himself with a brief few minutes. 'What can you do with *that*?' whispers one of Screwtape's emissaries to him. 'Just a thought or two from the Gospel of the day. Never mind about the Epistles. Forget about the Old Testament. Give no thought to "the whole counsel of God". Something off the cuff will do.' It certainly will; but do what?

If the tempter's voice is listened to, if in too many churches for too long a time such advice is followed,

8

what will happen? The results are easy to see. We shall rear a generation of Christians accustomed to the Eucharist but foreigners to many of the great truths of the Christian faith. They have never had the opportunity of listening, Sunday by Sunday, to a steady, intelligent, interesting exposition of the things most surely believed among us. They have been fed with snippets, little its and bits, nice thoughts for the day, but nothing, or practically nothing, from which bones and spiritual tissue can be built. Having never tasted strong meat, they go out into a questioning world ill equipped to answer questions. Their mouths, like the mouth of the River St Lawrence in winter, are frozen. They dare not speak, lest they make fools of themselves. They cannot witness—at least with their lips. They are spiritual Peter Pans.

If, in fact, this is what is happening, then I want to utter a warning, with the greatest possible urgency. But rather than do it myself, I will call in the aid of the prophet Amos to do it for me. You will recall how he was prophesying disaster for his people. How could he depict the greatest possible disaster that could befall a nation? This is, in fact, how he did it:

> 'Behold, the days are coming', says the Lord God,
> 'when I will send a famine on the land;
> not a famine of bread, nor a thirst for water,
> but of hearing the words of the Lord.
> They shall wander from sea to sea, and from north to east;
> they shall run to and fro, to seek the word of the Lord,
> but they shall not find it.' (8. 11-12, RSV)

This, in the mind of the prophet, is ultimate disaster for a nation. This is not, of course, the language of the politicians. Ultimate disaster in their reckoning is a rise

in the cost of living—Woe unto you, if you do not vote
for us, your steaks and your oil and your butter will rise
in price, your garages will have only one car instead of
two or three, your television will be black and white and
not coloured. This is ultimate disaster. The prophet
mentions none of these things. He knew that man did not
live by *these;* he lived by the Word of the Lord. Suppose
that that could not be obtained? Suppose there was
nobody to convey it? Suppose that the prophets gave the
people pretty little snippets and not the Word of the
Lord? Or suppose that the people were so deaf that they
could not receive the Word, even when it was delivered?
That, that would be disaster. That was the message of the
Lord to the Israel of Amos' day.

Today, in this last quarter of the twentieth century, there
is a craving for God. This, from one point of view, is the
more surprising when we consider the scientific sophistica-
tion of the previous decades of the century. As I wrote in
the Ashe Lecture:

> During them, man has ventured out into space, taken
> his first timid steps on the moon, and started to explore
> the universe in person. Man has 'come of age'—the
> phrase so beloved by Bonhoeffer has been taken up by
> a posse of theologians and expounded (though some-
> times in ways of which he himself might well have
> disapproved). Why bother about God? Has not the
> time come when He can be discounted? Is not the very
> idea of Him a relic of a pre-scientific age?
>
> Yet these are the very years in which we have
> witnessed a strange feeling after Him if haply men
> might find Him. Great numbers of our young people,
> sitting loose to, or even spurning, the orthodoxies of
> the established churches, have felt the emptiness, the

10

awful void, of an existence limited to what a material-
istic creed can offer. They have sought for something
deeper in the mysticism of the East, or for the ex-
periences which can be induced by the use of drugs.
They have refused—and how right they have been!—
to restrict the use of the word 'obscene' to the realm of
the sexual, and, with a clarity of vision sometimes
denied to their elders, have used the word of racism or
of the despoliation of Nature through an upsetting of
the ecological balance or a defilement of the air or the
sea. They may have no clearly defined doctrine of
creation such as would satisfy a Christian theologian,
but they have a clear perception of the blasphemy
occasioned by an atomic bomb or by a Sharpeville.[1]

If this craving, this search for God, be a fact (as I am
convinced it is in the case of multitudes of thinking
people today), it pinpoints the need for the multiplication
of places where it is known that there may be had what I
have described as intelligent, interesting, exposition of
the things most surely believed among us. When that
exposition has been given, and with it full opportunity
for discussion and debate, it may or may not be received,
welcomed, and lived by. *That* is not the final responsibility
of the preacher. *His* task is to see that it is available, and
that he is there to be the medium of it.

We shall be turning later in these lectures to some
biblical examples of preachers. But here today I would
take a preliminary look at one Old Testament figure who
has a particular word for us in the context of what I have
been saying in this opening lecture. Hosea, that broken-
hearted patriot, grieving over the faithlessness of his
people—a faithlessness of which he had to speak in

---

[1]*Convictions* (Hodder & Stoughton 1975; paperback 1978), p.24.

marital and sexual terms against the darkness of his own wife's desertion—Hosea pinpoints the reason for his nation's defection as 'lack of knowledge'. When he uses the word 'knowledge' he does not mean mere intellectual awareness, still less technological achievement. He means that knowledge of God which can only be interpreted in terms of obedience and love. 'There is no knowledge of God in the land' (4.1). 'My people are destroyed for lack of knowledge' (4.6). 'I desire steadfast love and not sacrifice, the knowledge of God rather than burnt offerings' (6.6). And so on. God had made himself known through a Jacob at Bethel and spoken with him (12.4); through a Moses in the delivery from Egypt (12.13), and that in the most intimate way—for, it should be noted, the same word is used for the knowledge of God as is used for the sexual 'knowledge' of a man and woman within marriage.

But at whose feet does Hosea lay the responsibility for his nation's lack of knowledge of God and for their defection from his worship? There can be no doubt of the answer. Priests and prophets, who should have been the agents of God's revelation, the bearers of his word, *they* are responsible, and it is their candle which will be removed.

> But it is not for any man to bring a charge,
> it is not for him to prove a case;
> the quarrel with you, false priest, is mine.
>
> Priest? By day and night you blunder on,
> you and the prophet with you.
> My people are ruined for lack of knowledge;
> your own countrymen are brought to ruin.
> You have rejected knowledge,
> and I will reject you from serving me as priest.

12

You have forgotten the teaching of God,
and I, your God, will forget your sons.

(Hosea 4. 4-6, NEB)

Hosea confronts us with a question, us who are the religious leaders in an age, albeit a wistful age, of spiritual ignorance and of moral decadence. It is a question which I propose to you as I propose it, with a measure of disquiet, to myself. It is this: How far are we to blame for the moral chaos and for the religious 'adultery' of our country today? I do not know the answer. But in seeking to find it, I find myself compelled to ask how much solid, systematic, down-to-earth and up-to-heaven teaching goes on in our churches? What have we to say about divine law, not to speak of divine grace? When did we last expound the Ten Commandments, or so deal with the Sermon on the Mount as to make our listeners cry out, 'Lord, have mercy upon us, and incline our hearts to keep this law'? Have we been guilty, in the euphoria which springs from seeing an increase in the number of acts of communion made, of having a share in producing a generation of Christians ignorant of the rudiments of the Christian faith and unable intelligently to share it with others?

Let me close with two quotations—the first from that faithful adherent of the Anglican *via media*, John Donne, one-time Dean of St Paul's Cathedral, London: 'If there be a discontinuing or slackening of preaching, there is the danger of losing Christ'.

The second quotation comes from a modern writer, Dr Vance Havner:

I think preachers are getting lost in a multitude of smaller duties. The preacher has a peculiar place in the economy of God. He is in danger of becoming so involved with secondary affairs that he loses his prophetic gift. The devil doesn't care how great a success a preacher is in any other field, if he can just kill the prophet in him.

2

A Non-Prophet Organization?

What the Lord says to me,
that I will speak.

2 A Non-Prophet Organization?

The first lecture sounded a sombre note. It hinted at the possibility that, in the words of *The Gospel according to Peanuts*[1], the Church might become 'the world's largest non-prophet organisation'. God forbid, for that would mean the removal of its candle from its place, the spewing of it from the mouth of God as something tepid, lukewarm, futile.

Let me seek, in these second and third lectures, to strike a more positive note, and invite you to share with me in some Bible study. We shall examine together a cross-section of the prophetic figures of the Bible, briefly, and more by way of invitation to further study than in any exhaustive fashion.

But first, what is it that constitutes a prophet, that marks him out from other men who have other tasks to perform in society? I should like to begin to give an answer to that question in the words of Jacques Ellul, that perceptive writer whose book *The Politics of God and the Politics of Man*[2] gives many fresh insights into the meaning of the Old Testament. He is looking into the question of what it was that made Elisha a prophet.

> What constitutes the prophet (he writes) is exact and rigorous proclamation of what God does, of God's decision, today. With objectivity, with, one might almost say, a certain indifference, a detachment as if it were no concern of his, the prophet says: 'Look, God has decided this'. But it is not just this unveiling (revelation) of the intention of God that makes a man a

[1] Robert L. Short (Collins Fontana 1966), p.25.
[2] Eerdmans, Grand Rapids, Mich., new edition 1972.

prophet. It is also the proclamation of an order: 'Listen to the Word of God'. There is something more important than trying to engage in trade, or to support oneself, or to watch on the walls, or to punish criminals: stop all that. Listen, now, to God's Word. The prophet offers a living Word for the present. He offers a Word relevant to the actual situation of men, a Word which will be a solution, but which is completely irrational and unexpected, and which implies for man a strange renouncing of his own methods and policies and normal inclinations. The prophet is in effect the man who brings a Word of God to bear on the actual, concrete situation of man, his political situation.

Now, if this is true, the prophet is, *par excellence*, the man with a burden. His is not, like Christian's in Bunyan's *Pilgrim's Progress,* the burden of his sin. The preacher, if indeed he is the preacher of good news, has been to the Cross and left his burden there. He knows where to go when he must rid himself of that kind of burden. No: he is a man burdened with a message.

The word 'burden' is, of course, a biblical one, and is deeply significant. It seems to convey a typically Hebrew insight. It occurs frequently in the Old Testament prophetic literature (any biblical dictionary will give you the instances). The Septuagint misses the point of the word, for it translates it by comparatively colourless words, such as *lemma* and *rema* which simply mean 'a word', and *horasis* and *horama* which mean 'a vision'. But the Hebrew word means what it says—a load, a burden, something which weighs on a man. Now a burden is what somebody puts on your shoulders, or which you take on yourself, and which it is your task to deliver— you must not free yourself of it till you have delivered it where it is destined to go. That precisely is what it means to be a prophet.

Now, a man in such a position as this—burdened, weighed down with a word of the Lord—is not miserable, because, in Christian terms, his word is good news even though it includes judgement. Indeed he has a great and joyful sympathy with St Paul: 'I cannot help myself; it would be misery to me *not* to preach' (1 Cor. 9.16, NEB). But he can never be a flippant man. He can never be a trifler. He has a weighty word to deliver.

Let us see how this works out in certain specific Biblical instances.

I

The story of *Micaiah*, son of Imlah, is told in 1 Kings 22, and told brilliantly. Here are two kings, the King of Israel and Jehoshaphat the King of Judah, entering into an agreement with one another to put an end by war to the situation whereby the King of Syria has possession of Ramoth-Gilead. Jehoshaphat, perhaps slightly ill at ease about the affair, suggests that enquiry first be made for the word of the Lord. The King of Israel agrees—it is nice to have your tanks and submarines blessed by the Church! The prophets gather—quite an array of them, some 400 all told. Prominent among them is Zedekiah, son of Chenaanah, who speaks on behalf of all the prophets and does so dramatically by making horns of iron to illustrate how the Syrians were to be pushed out into destruction when the two kings attacked them. Quite a gesture! One can hear the purring of satisfaction from kings and prophets alike.

Still the conscience of the King of Israel seems ill at ease. Almost against his own desire, he mentions to

Jehoshaphat that there is one prophet known to him—
and hated by him—who has not appeared with the
400, Micaiah son of Imlah, an unpopular figure, 'for he
never prophesies good concerning me, but evil' (v. 8).
He is summoned into the presence, the messenger warning him en route that all the 400 have encouraged war
and he had better do the same (v. 13). The question is
put to him: 'Shall we go to battle or not?' (v. 15). The
very tone of his reply makes it plain to the King that
Micaiah did not mean a word of what he said; he meant
in fact the direct contrary—'Go up and triumph; the
Lord will give it into the hand of the King'. The King
adjures the prophet to speak the truth. 'I saw all Israel',
said the prophet, 'scattered upon the mountains. . . .' 'I
told you so', said the King, 'he always prophesies evil.'
But Micaiah elaborates his judgement: the prophets have
been enticed, the whole bunch of them. They have lied.
God has not spoken through them. Only disaster awaits
the Kings if they pursue their ill-conceived design.
Zedekiah may smite Micaiah on the cheek (did not
Jesus, the greatest of the prophets, suffer in just such
fashion?); the King of Israel may have Micaiah thrust
into prison and have him fed with bread and water (did
not Peter undergo similar treatment?); but it will not
avert the sure disaster which Micaiah has prophesied.

It is a dramatic episode, and full of meaning and of
warning for those in any age who are entrusted with the
Word of the Lord. It says to us that the true prophet will
probably have to endure loneliness and censure even in
the house of those who might be expected to be his
friends. Micaiah was a man who refused to jump on the
popular band-wagon, even though that band-wagon was
a completely ecclesiastical one. It is hard enough to
stand out against 'the world'—Athanasius *contra mundum*;

20

how much more difficult to stand out *contra ecclesiam*!

Micaiah provides the preacher at once with a motto and a prayer: 'As the Lord lives, what the Lord says to me, that I will speak' (v. 14). Prophetic boldness involves loneliness and suffering; and the pages of history are strewn with the stories of men of God who, at any cost, have stood by that stern and demanding motto.

II

Our second instance—and I am not worrying about chronological order here—is that of *Jeremiah*. Here was a man with a burden, if ever there was one. Reticent, diffident, unwilling to be a public figure (1. 4-10), he came under the divine compulsion as 'the Lord stretched out his hand and touched my mouth, and said to me, "I put my words into your mouth".' But it was to be a costly ministry—bonds and imprisonment were to await him.

The whole prophecy should be studied, to get the story and feel the atmosphere. Here I will refer you to only two passages:-

(*a*) Chapter 20. Jeremiah's opponents are found in the house of those who should be his friends. Pashur son of Immer the priest was 'the chief officer in the house of the Lord', and should surely have been an ally to this sensitive man of God. On the contrary, he had him flogged and put in prison for a night. Jeremiah, released, turns on him, renames him 'Terror let loose' *(Magor-Missabib)* and prophesies disaster both for the people of Judah by their deportation to Babylon and for *Terror let loose* and his family. Then, physically and nervously exhausted, Jeremiah turns to the Lord, turns *on* the Lord:

21

O Lord, thou hast duped me, and I have been thy
  dupe;
Thou hast outwitted me and hast prevailed (v. 7).

Have you ever spoken to God like that? No, you may
reply; I would not be so blasphemous. Well, blasphemy
it may be. But if I may put it crudely, I think it is the kind
of blasphemy which God understands. The Psalmists
had a way of turning on God sometimes and asking him
why he didn't wake up (e.g. 44.23). Job had a way of
complaining. If you have thoughts 'kindled in hell within
you', far better blurt them out to a Father who understands
than let them smoulder on in inner resentment (see
Frank Lake, *Clinical Theology*[1], p. 369).

Jeremiah goes on complaining (vv. 7 and 8)—he is a
laughing-stock, mocked for uttering the Word of the
Lord. Would it not be better (v. 9) to forget about God
altogether, never to speak in his name again? (Wouldn't
it be nice to have free week-ends, and a conscience that
just didn't register.) But he cannot bring himself to do
any such thing. When the idea entered his head, then
God's Word was imprisoned in his body, like a fire
blazing in his heart, and he was weary with holding it
under, and could endure no more (v. 9).

The fire in his heart! The hammer in his hand! The
burden which he must deliver—or burst! This is the
mark of the prophet.

(*b*) The second passage is Jeremiah 23. The chapter
consists of a study in contrast—between true prophets
and false. The picture of a false prophet, so vividly given
here, throws into relief the lineaments of the true. The
true prophet is the one who 'has stood in the council of
the Lord' (v. 18; the phrase recurs in v. 22)—there is a

[1]Darton, Longman, and Todd 1966.

22

phrase whose meaning is worth pondering. Did you 'stand in the council of the Lord' before you preached last Sunday, to see him, to hear him, and to obey (v. 18)? The vision of God and the listening to God precede the speaking of the word of God. Only then comes the speaking, and then it must be done with utter faithfulness ('in truth', v. 28).

The closing verses of the chapter (vv. 33-40) are a searching indictment of those who lightly talk about the burden of the Lord and have no clue as to the meaning of that searching phrase.

III

Our third instance is that of *Amos*. We have referred to him, *en passant*, in the first lecture. A slightly more careful look at him is called for now. He was a man with a totally 'un-clerical' background. He came of no prophetic line; his forebears and he himself were small farmers (7. 14 ff). He was a rustic. While young Isaiah was mixing with the court, young Amos was looking after sheep and dressing sycamore-figs. He came from the inconsiderable village of Tekoa in a narrow ravine surrounded by hills overlooking the Dead Sea, the sort of lonely country where prophets can meet with God and be made. Those years tending the cattle were years of preparation, in which the fires began to burn, till they blazed so hot that he had to leave the farm and 'go prophesy'.

If his message lacked the tenderness of Hosea's, it reflected the sternness of his geographical surroundings. His message, his burden, was one of almost unrelieved judgement. There is 'scarcely a sob in his voice'. Perhaps he was nearer John Baptist than Jesus—plenty of truth, but not very much grace. But his message was greatly needed. I mention two of its outstanding features.

(*a*) *He condemns thoughtless luxury and national softness* (e.g. in 4. 1-3; 5. 10-15; 6. 1-7). Amos said to the men of his day, as he would say especially today to the prosperous nations of the West: Material prosperity is not the main criterion by which to judge the welfare of a nation or of an individual. As I have written elsewhere: 'There is needed a revolt—and who better to initiate and foster it than the Christian disciple?—a revolt against the violence which rapacity breeds, against the creed of giantism ("the bigger the thing, be it organization or motor car or profit, the better"), against the prodigality of a society which puts profit before people, and which is prepared to rape and violate nature provided that luxury is promoted. *This* is obscenity; we are at last learning not to restrict the use of that word to a sexual context. It is obscene to pollute the earth, the air, the water. It is obscene to allow twenty per cent of the world's people to own eighty per cent of its capital resources. It is obscene to give the verb to grasp, to acquire, to possess, precedence over the verb to be.'[1]

(*b*) *He condemns unethical religion* (e.g. in 2. 6ff; 4. 4-5; 5. 21-4; etc.). 'The rank incense of a religion that was without morality' (to use George Adam Smith's phrase) stank in the nostrils of Yahweh.

With almost terrible directness, Jesus takes up the point in the Sermon on the Mount (Matthew 5. 23-4)—if you have a wrong relationship with somebody and recall it as you are going to church, give your church-going a miss for the moment, get that relationship right, and then back to church you go. Until that is put right,

[1]The Shaftesbury Lecture (1973) 'Some Christian Convictions for the Twentieth Century', p. 9. Quoted from my *Convictions,* op. cit., p. 202. The theme is worked out with some care in J. V. Taylor's *Enough is Enough,* (SCM Press 1975).

church-going is a mockery. Unethical religion stinks in the nostrils of God.

Perhaps it was, at least in part, the desert which gave Amos such clarity of vision, that gave this layman from the working classes, this recruit from common life, such surety of spiritual touch. Many of us (most of us?) lack that background and lack that perspicacity. How blind 'religious' people have been down the years to moral issues, and how often they have become the victims of unethical religion! It took the Church many centuries to see the evils of slavery and to shake the system to its foundations—though the principles which would undermine it were written into the New Testament documents. Today we 'religious' people have our blind spots in ethical matters, some of us acquiescing in racial intolerance, others in carelessness about the conditions in the third world, others prepared to tolerate conditions which treat women as second-class creatures. You name it—maybe I have it.

But the strength of Amos, a strength which enabled him to face even Amaziah, that Old Testament Caiaphas (7. 10 ff), sprang not only from the desert but also, and mainly, from the conviction that he was a man called by God to prophesy. 'I am no prophet, nor the son of a prophet . . . but the Lord took me . . . and the Lord said to me "Go, prophesy . . . ".' 'On such words we do not comment;' wrote George Adam Smith, 'we do them homage.'

There have, of course, been many like him, down the centuries of the Church's life. Peter dares to see that Cornelius is not unclean (Acts 10). James the conservative perceives that the Gentiles are in on God's plan of salvation. Martin Luther cries out: 'Here I stand, I can no other'. Dietrich Bonhoeffer, who could so easily have

25

sheltered in America, goes to his death in Germany—
'this is the end; for me the beginning'. Beyers Naudé
wages his weary battle in South Africa because he sees
that all men stand equal before God, whatever their
pigmentation may be. Solzhenitsyn and Alan Paton
write—and find their pens mightier than the sword.

'The goodly fellowship of the prophets praise Thee.'

IV

The greatness of *Hosea* (to whom I referred briefly in my
first lecture) came through his passion. He became the
prophet that he was through entering into the meaning
of the suffering God. He can well be described as the
broken-hearted patriot of Israel.

The Bible is rich in patriotism. One thinks of Moses,
willing to be blotted out of God's book if by that means
the well-nigh unforgiveable sin of his nation's apostasy
could thereby be expunged (Exod. 32. 30-5); or of St
Paul who 'could almost pray that I myself were accursed
and cut off from Christ for the sake of my brethren, my
kinsmen by race' (Romans 9. 3). Or again—and
supremely—one thinks of Jesus, weeping over Jerusalem
(Luke 19. 41 ff).

Hosea's patriotism sprang from the depths of the
bitterness of his personal and family tragedy, his experience of love spurned and thrown back in his face. It
is this experience which gives to his religious patriotism
its depth and passion. As Wheeler Robinson poignantly
wrote: 'It was one thing to hold in general that God
loved Israel; it was another to have that knowledge
confirmed by the analogy of his own experience and to

know that God *so* loved Israel as Hosea found himself loving Gomer'.[1] 'Hosea's power was in his wound.'[2]

Some have taken the story of Gomer's unfaithfulness as an allegory. I doubt this very much. I believe we have in this story flesh and blood matrimonial tragedy. Probably the first child born to him was indeed his own (1.3); the second (1. 6—'she who never knew a father's pity') and the third (1. 8-9—'not my people') illegitimate. As Hosea, broken-hearted, pondered and brooded, he tried to make sense out of this nonsensical tragedy. God took this fearful minus, and made it into a plus. The essence of a gospel emerged. The nation was—Gomer. It was forsaking its true Husband for the local baals; it was a harlot, selling herself to be fertilized by others. With a change of imagery, Hosea sees the nation as a disobedient child (11. 1-4); picture is piled on picture, to paint, in colours as lurid as may be, the scene of defection and of unrequited love. The result of such sin can be seen in the decay, both moral and political, which has set into the bones of the nation; political judgement is warped because moral judgement has gone by default.

Hosea does more than denounce. He can see an answer to this national tragedy. It lies in the knowledge of God (4. 6, etc.), and in that turning to him which is in fact a child's home-coming to its Father. Israel has sinned not only against law but against love. Hosea looked into his own heart and found it broken because of Gomer's unfaithfulness. He looked into the heart of God and found it a broken heart, too.

It was *this* that made him the preacher he was—and, for that matter, is.

[1] *Two Hebrew Prophets* (Lutterworth 1948), p.25.
[2] Ibid., p.29.

If Hosea's greatness as a prophet came through his passion, Isaiah's greatness came through his vision of the holiness of God.

Isaiah was as much at home in the city as Amos was in the country. He moved, apparently, in the circles of leadership in Jerusalem. Perhaps he himself was a courtier. It is to his credit that, mixing in those circles, he maintained his spiritual life at such a level as enabled him to receive a vision and hear a voice.

Isaiah 6 tells the story, when read in conjunction with 2 Chronicles 26, of the fall of an idol. For fifty-two long years Uzziah had reigned, and a magnificent reign it had been. The Chronicler tells of his power and energy in some detail and with obvious admiration. But pride came before a fall which was all the greater because of the length and brilliance of the reign which preceded it. Daring to undertake a task which belonged to the priests alone, Uzziah was struck down with leprosy where he stood, hard by the altar. He rushed from the temple—to die a leper's death, in a separate house.

It was a moment of disillusionment, of disenchantment for young Isaiah, as he pondered on the death of his hero-king. But in the very year, that *annus terribilis,* the year of the old king's death, Isaiah saw another King, higher, mightier than Uzziah, against whose purity the uncleanness of his erstwhile sovereign, of his nation, and—not least—of himself, stood out in aweful contrast.

Language is strained to the limit to describe the holiness of the King of kings. The temple shakes—the very temple which had been desecrated by Uzziah's act. The mysterious seraphim cover themselves. Smoke fills the house, the smoke which always arises when holiness and sin touch each other. The whole picture, the language of which has affected the New Testament and especially Revelation chapter 4, is full of awe.

Awe is a word too little heard today. Too easily we mortals assume a position of hand-shaking familiarity with God. 'Nothing is more needed in the Church today than a recovery of a sense of beyondness'.[1] Humiliation in the face of sin, personal and national, and a consciousness of guilt and of the need for the cauterizing ministry of cleansing, this must be the prelude to that encounter with God which makes it possible for the question to be heard: 'Whom shall I send?' and for the answer to be given: 'Here am I, send me'.

That is the *sine qua non* in the making of a preacher.

We turn from the Old Testament to the New; and first, to St Paul. The subject of St Paul as a prophet would require a book in itself, not part of one lecture. So here I confine myself to one verse or, rather, one half-verse in which, with extraordinary lucidity and brevity, he sums up what he sees to be the essentials of prophet-hood. I refer to 2 Corinthians 2. 17b (NEB).

The passage is clearly polemical; he is hitting out at some people who 'go hawking the word of God about'. What, or whom, exactly he has in mind is not clear to us (it doubtless was all too clear to them!); probably it was the popular preacher type at whom we looked when we were studying Micaiah's opponents. Let it rest at that.

Now let us look at the genuine article: 'when we declare the word we do it in sincerity, as from God and in God's sight, as members of Christ'.

Here we have four points to notice, four hall-marks of prophetic authenticity:

[1] John Taylor, *The Go-Between God* (SCM Press 1972).

(i) 'We declare the word . . . *in sincerity.*' We recall the word of the cynic: 'What you are speaks so loud that I cannot hear what you say'. Here in St Paul's dictum there is no cynicism; simply the positive statement: 'we do it in sincerity'.

Alan Paton's *Life* of Archbishop Clayton of Cape Town[1] is the moving story of a man who stood firm against apartheid precisely because he had the clarity of prophetic insight into the nature of God and of man, and the sincerity of heart to declare what he saw. His biographer writes this of his preaching:

> There were not many preachers of his calibre in England, or anywhere else for that matter. It was almost impossible for him to preach badly. He held his audience and congregations, not with any tricks nor with those gadgets he had so scathingly referred to, but with that authority, those considered judgements, those reports on his adopted country which somehow rang true, because it was very difficult to believe that this preacher could practise deception or self-deception; and all this delivered in those short sentences and simple words.[2]

Richard Baxter in his *Reformed Pastor*[3] (a book which Hensley Henson described as the finest book on pastoralia in the English language) wrote on similar lines:

> Take heed to yourselves lest your example contradict your doctrine, and lest you lay such stumbling-blocks before the blind as may be the occasion of their ruin: lest you unsay with your lives what you say with your tongues; and be the greatest hinderers of the success

[1] *Apartheid and the Archbishop: the Life and Times of Geoffrey Clayton* (Jonathan Cape 1974).

[2] Op. cit., p. 165.

[3] Rev. edn. (Epworth Press 1950), pp. 161-2.

of your own labours. It much hindereth our work when other men are all the week long contradicting to poor people in private that which we have been speaking to them from the Word of God in public, because we cannot be at hand to expose their folly; but it will much more hinder if we contradict ourselves, and if our actions give our tongue the lie, and if you build up an hour or two with your mouths, and all the week after pull down with your hands! This is the way to make men think that the Word of God is but an idle tale, and to make preaching seem no better than prating. He that means as he speaks, will sure do as he speaks.

(ii) 'We declare the word . . . *as from God*'. We need say little about this, for we have noted this carefully, for example in the case of Amos of whom we said that his 'strength sprang . . . mainly from the conviction that he was a man called by God to prophesy'. It is a recurring theme in St Paul. He states it militantly at the beginning of the Epistle to the Galatians: 'Paul, an apostle, not by human appointment or human commission, but by commission from Jesus Christ and from God the Father who raised him from the dead' (1. 1).

For the present-day preacher this does not mean that he is constantly harking back to his original 'call'—'God called me in 1928' or whenever. Rather, when we dare to say that 'we declare the word . . . as from God', we mean that there is, here and now, communication between God and us. In some sense, however dim the realization of it may be, we live 'in the secret place of the Most High'. From that place we go with a word from God to the people.

(iii) 'We declare the word . . . *in God's sight*'. However

small the congregation may be to which we preach, however undistinguished, however unappreciative or irresponsive, there is One there 'in whose sight' we preach. The King of kings is in the congregation. We cannot prate or strut before *him*. We are always under judgement, the searching, kindly judgement of One whose we are and whom we serve. We do our work 'in God's sight'.

(iv) 'We declare the word . . . *as members of Christ*'. When the preacher stands in the pulpit, he does not stand as a pathetic, lone figure. He stands there as part of the Body of Christ, engaging in an activity of the Church which is the redeemed and the redeeming community. I have written of this elsewhere.[1] Here I can only say that, when preaching takes place, the Gospel prolongs itself, and the hearers enter into partnership with the preacher, co-operating with him in prayer, their minds erect to grasp what God has to say, and their wills set to obey.

So the Church is built up, the man in the pulpit and the people in the pew working together 'as members of Christ' for the edifying of the Body.

As we turn now to look at the figure of Jesus as a preacher, we see all the main characteristics of those whom we have already studied *subsumed* in him. Briefly let me sketch what you might care to work out in more detailed study.

Micaiah, fearless in facing the civil and ecclesiastical leaders of his day. 'As the Lord lives, what the Lord says to me, that I will speak.' *Jesus*, rebuking 'that fox', denouncing the religious hypocrites, scorning religious language which covers irreligious conduct.

[1]See my *Stewards of Grace* (Hodder and Stoughton 1958), chapter 7.

Jeremiah, coming all-unwillingly under the divine compulsion, as 'the Lord stretched out his hand and touched my mouth'. *Jesus,* driven by the Spirit into the wilderness and impelled by an ever-recurring 'must'—to be about his Father's business, to suffer and to die. . . . The passion of Jeremiah is 'fulfilled' in Jesus, and his cry 'O Lord, thou hast duped me' is reflected at a deeper level in the cry of dereliction, 'My God, my God, why hast thou forsaken me?'.

Amos coming from the desert, *Jesus* from the country town and the desert-temptation. Amos with the conviction that 'the Lord took me . . . and the Lord said to me, "Go, prophesy" '; *Jesus* ever mindful of the Baptism experience, and the voice that said: 'This is my beloved Son, in whom I am well pleased'.

Hosea, the broken-hearted patriot, grieving over an adulterous nation; *Jesus* weeping over the beloved city: 'O Jerusalem, Jerusalem, the city that murders the prophets and stones the messengers sent to her! How often have I longed to gather your children, as a hen gathereth her brood under her wings; but you would not let me.'

Isaiah with his vision of the dazzling holiness of a King greater than Uzziah; *Jesus* with his teaching of the King whose will must be done and whose Kingdom must come.

All is subsumed in Jesus. The greatest of the prophets is here. In him we reach the climax of the prophetic line. He 'fulfilled' the prophets. He surpassed the prophets. If what we have seen of the Old Testament prophets and of St Paul could be summed up as a *study of obedience to a divine imperative,* here in Jesus we see an obedience which transcends theirs. Here was total obedience, even unto death. It is the unknown writer of the Epistle to the Hebrews who works out this theme in greater detail than any other of the New Testament writers. He does so especially in chapter 10, with the repetition of the words from Psalm 40, 'Lo, I have come to do thy will', and the application of these words to our Lord in his offering of himself once for all. This was a sacrifice which transcended all animal sacrifices to the point where they became but a feeble shadow of the reality in Christ. The language is hinted at again in St Paul's Epistle to the Philippians— 'he humbled himself and became obedient unto death, even death on a cross' (2. 8).

But if we continue to compare the persons and work of the prophets with the person and work of Jesus, the comparison only throws into relief the greatness of Jesus. We have briefly noticed, for example, the pressure—it is hard to find a better word for it than this—the pressure and sense of divine constraint under which the prophets worked. They described it variously:- Amos in terms of a divine word which came to him; Jeremiah in terms of fire and hammer; Ezekiel in terms of a hand pressing on him (3. 22; 33. 22, etc.), and so on. In the Gospels that note is there, all the stronger for the reticence of the language used in describing it. There was a divine 'must' in the life and ministry of Jesus (St John is particularly fond of the word, e.g. 3. 14; 4. 4; 9. 4; 10. 16; 12. 34; 20. 9). There is a 'driving' of the Spirit which must not be refused (with Luke 4. 1 cp. Romans 8. 14). There is a baptism to be baptized with (Luke 12. 50), and a terrible constraint 'until the ordeal is over' (NEB). Here is a divine imperative at work, a divine pressure if ever there was one, and an obedience total and complete. It is all the more remark-able that it seems to have been accompanied by an astonishing serenity, only broken on occasion by an overwhelming sense of man's sin and folly and, at the end, by the awful burden he had to bear.

There is another feature in the ministry of Jesus which we must notice, and here again there seems to be a contrast with that of the prophets. The ministry of the word in the life-work of Jesus, the teaching and preaching task, went hand in hand with the ministry of healing, healing both of diseased bodies and of distressed minds. Sometimes, indeed, the healing took place by a word spoken by Jesus at a distance from the patient (see e.g. Matthew 8. 5-13). But generally word and healing action went together. We must remember that, in a subject nation and in days when there was no Welfare State provision for the sick, conditions must have been appalling. But I notice that Jesus never succumbed to the temptation to doff the preacher's robe and become a social worker. He never allowed himself to be confronted with the choice between social work and preaching, *either* one *or* the other. Not at all. Ministry of word and ministry of healing touch went together.

Is there a message here for the twentieth-century Church? Is there a word to those who have lost their confidence in the power of the Word and been tempted to go into social service? And a message, too, to those who fail to realize that the Lord of the Church has committed to his followers a ministry of healing? Word and touch were joined together in the ministry of Jesus as apparently they were not in that of the prophets before him. What he has joined together, let no man put asunder.

So we could go on comparing the preaching ministry of the prophets with that of our Lord and in doing so we should only discover his incomparable greatness.

But there is one final sphere in which there can be no

comparison, only contrast. It lies here. The prophets saw their life-work as being that of men who *bore* to others the word of God. Jesus *was* the Word of God. Here comparisons end. Here is uniqueness.

The classic exposition of this theme is, of course, to be found in the Prologue to the Fourth Gospel. There is a long and complicated background to this profound passage, as all of you know. (A reading, for example, of C. H. Dodd on the Fourth Gospel shows just how complicated that background was.) There are phrases in the canonical and non-canonical writings which pull one up short and make one think. For example, the writer of the Book of Wisdom (18.15-16) can speak of God's eternal word 'leaping from heaven, from the royal throne'. St Luke, in the preface to his Gospel, can use the strange phrase 'eye-witnesses . . . of the word' (1. 2) in a semi-personal sense. St Paul, in the first chapter of the Epistle to the Colossians, can give us a Christology of enormous power, comparable with the majesty of that found in the first chapter of the Epistle to the Hebrews. *But* it is only in the Prologue to the Fourth Gospel that we have the stark, almost brutal affirmation: 'The Word was made flesh and tabernacled among us' (1.14). No wonder that Lancelot Andrewes, faced by this astonishing statement, exclaimed in awe: 'The Word, and unable to speak a word!'.

Something greater than the prophets is here; something infinitely greater! Oh come, let us adore him, Christ the Word.

3

To be a Pointer

I only pray that, as I voice the message,
Men may find God.

3   To be a Pointer

The title of this lecture is not Bunyan's famous words 'to be a pilgrim' but 'to be a pointer'. Let me clarify what I have in mind.

When a man has been at the job of preaching for a good many years, he does well to look back and review; to think of the many hours which he has spent in preparation—reading, studying, thinking, writing—as well as in travelling (if his ministry has been, like mine, of a peripatetic nature) and in the actual delivery of what he has prepared. Look at those notes, piles and piles of them. Words, words, more words!

What has been the purpose of this herculean labour? What has he been trying to do down the years? Has he been trying to prop up an institution, to perpetuate a venerable practice into the late twentieth century? Has he been declaiming an ideology? Quite frankly, I am not over-interested in doing these things. Some practices, good in their day, are best left to history; let them be buried as relics of the past. And as for ideologies, the world is full of these, and there is no lack of men and women to expound them.

But if, on the other hand, the preacher has, over the years, been seeking to uncover the truth as it has been made known in Jesus, the truth about God and man and society and eternity, the mighty acts of God's redeeming love and the creative and re-creative work of the Holy Spirit—if this has been his purpose, then, I say, every moment of his work has been time well spent.

For this is a theme so deep in its mystery, so vast in its ramifications, so penetrating in its relevance to belief and practice, that one short life and the experience of one mere mortal will only serve to touch its fringe.

Which leads me to a matter which, I believe, is of great importance to the preacher.

There are those who tell us that we should only preach what we know to be true in our own experience. They certainly have a point here. They are in fact appealing for honesty in the pulpit—no high-falutin' phrases, no airy-fairy claims for the faith which won't stand up to the rigours of human experience, no hot air in homiletics. Good. The point is well made. If I do not personally know the meaning of divine forgiveness, my sermon on that theme will have a hollow ring about it. If I preach eloquently on the peace of God while every line on my face bears witness to a life of acute and obsessive anxiety, then I may have produced a polished essay but I can hardly claim to have *preached* on this theme.

But we cannot leave it at that. For if I preach only what I have experienced, then my hearers will have to live on an impoverished diet. I am not a giant in the things of God, nor indeed are most of us who occupy the pulpits of our churches. Even if we were an Anselm or a Chrysostom, a Luther or a Wesley, a Newman or a Temple, there are limits to one man's experience, and his grasp of truth is bound to be to some extent one-sided. We all have our favourite themes which tend to throw out of proportion the many-sided truth of God. We need others to set our balance right.

Thank God, this is precisely what we have. I am only one, a rather insignificant one, of a great host of men and women who, over long millennia, have known God, loved God, served God, worshipped God, experienced God in far richer and profounder fashion than I am ever likely to do. I am, thank God, part of the one holy catholic and apostolic Church. 'The glorious company of the apostles praise thee. The goodly fellowship of the prophets praise thee. The noble army of martyrs praise thee.' There are riches here.

So I learn, as a preacher, to become a *pointer*. The Canadian Rockies have held for me a kind of alluring fascination since I first saw them in the early forties. I'm not much of a climber. I know something of the exhilaration that comes from the fresh air on the lower slopes. I may even have had a go at a peak or two. Maybe with experience I might climb some of the higher peaks. But there are other men, far greater climbers than I, who have been much higher, ventured far more nobly, and discovered things which I can only faintly guess at. Let me introduce you to them, that in some way at least you may share their experience and catch their vision. That's what the saints are for. That's what the theologians are for. That's what the great explorers, of truth and experience and labour, are for; and even they have never got to the very top of those Rockies of Christian truth. Only One ever did that, and I want to point to *him*. But of that, more anon.

Yes, I will preach to the limits of my experience of God in Christ. If I have not *something* in that field, I cannot preach at all. But I will preach beyond the limits of my experience. I believe in the one, holy, catholic, and apostolic Church. And I believe in the communion of saints.

After writing these paragraphs, I read the proofs of Colin Morris's book *The Word and the Words*[1]. He has a worthwhile passage on this theme:

> Making personal experience a basic criterion by which true preaching is judged is to run the risk of an unhealthy and cramped subjectivism. No preacher can live more

[1]Epworth Press 1975.

than one life, experience more than a finite number of situations, know more things than one brain can contain. So from his own resources he cannot speak to the clamant needs of any congregation, however small it may be. Hence, the Church. . . .

The Church is the greatest preacher in Christian history and the individual preacher preaches *to* the Church from the Gospel in order that he may preach *from* the Church to the world. Put differently: the preacher can only preach beyond his own experience when he is preaching out of the Church's. And what a rich tapestry can be woven from the history of the universal Church! Could anything befall mortal man that the Church has not known? Bane and blessing, pain and pleasure, glory and defeat, humiliation and vindication, betrayal and forgiveness—the Church has lived through the totality of human experience. So the preacher's 'We' is neither editorial nor royal; it is confessional. 'Were you there when they crucified my Lord?' asks the spiritual. To which the preacher can answer 'Yes!'; *and* when the Holy Spirit in tongues of flame licked a motley assembly at Pentecost into shape—the form of the primitive Church; *and* at every historical crisis precipitated by the Gospel ever since.

Hence, there must always be a dialectical relationship between the preacher and the Church. He can attack or defend it, but in the last resort he must affirm it. Sometimes the preacher's attitude towards the Church may be one of questioning or even disillusionment; at others, his understanding of the Gospel may lead him to repudiate it. But the tension is always there. The Church haunts the heretic as the memory of home teases the Prodigal. It is the datum-point, the landmark on the map from which the preacher gets his bearings. The Church and the preacher's need of each other is mutual. In the preacher, the Church becomes conscious of itself. In the Church, the preacher draws upon a fount of living faith immeasurably greater than his own.

Canon D. W. Cleverley Ford, who has done more for the preaching of the Church of England than any other man in this generation, entitled one of his books: *Have you anything to declare?*[1] It is a brilliant and searching title, taken, of course, from the Customs. The book is, in a sense, autobiographical. In it, he tells of how Christ became to him a reality, of how membership of the Church deepened that experience, of how scholarship and especially the critical study of the Bible enriched it. He writes against the background of a long parochial and pastoral ministry. The main point of his book is that, if a man is to preach, he must hammer out for himself what he has to declare. This Ford does in his book, so far as he himself is concerned, and at the end finds he has something which pretty closely approximates to the main items of the Apostles' Creed. Each man must do this for himself, if his preaching is to be live preaching. It may be painful work, for belief is not always easily come by, especially in a world where pain and injustice abound and where the Christian sometimes feels constrained to cry out, as the Psalmist did, 'Wake up, O God, why are you asleep?' (Psalm 44. 23).

It would prove a wholesome exercise for those of us who engage in the ministry of the Word to sit down—and a good deal more than one sitting will be required for this operation—and think out, and write down, what are 'the things most surely believed' not only 'among us' but '*by me*'. What are the literally vital things in the Christian

[1] Mowbrays 1973.

gospel, so far as I am concerned? What do I live by? What would I die for, if it came to the point? What will I die by? It may well be that, at the end of such an operation, I shall find on my writing pad something short of the credal formularies of the Christian Church. There will be some items, some doctrines, more precious to me, more vital, than others. There may be some items which, at my present level of understanding, have not come very much alive to me and which, if I were foolish enough to do so, I could at present jettison. But at least I shall have a framework of belief. I shall have something to declare. On that, revisable from time to time, I shall be able to rear a super-structure of ever-increasing richness as the years go by, as experience widens and as reading and thinking extend.

There is, of course, an aspect of this matter on which so far I have not touched. There are the great 'securities of the Christian faith' with which the preacher is put in trust when he is ordained as a minister of God's Word and sacraments, and which he is to 'keep intact'. I use here Moffatt's translation of 1 Tim. 6.20 and 2 Tim. 1.14. The preacher is not a lone figure, preaching what appeals to him most and leaving the rest unsaid. He is, rather, the last in the apostolic line of those through whose preaching God's salvation in Christ continues. Through him the gospel reverberates. Those who know P. T. Forsyth's *Positive Preaching and the Modern Mind*[1] may recall his words: 'Preaching is the Gospel prolonging and declaring itself. The gift of God's grace was, and is, his work of Gospel. And it is this Act which is prolonged in the word of the preacher and not merely declared' (pp. 5 ff). Those of you who do *not* know this book, I beseech you to sell your collar and buy a copy. And if

[1]Hodder and Stoughton 1907.

44

perchance you cannot get it, or if—which God forbid!—it is too steep for you, then sell your pocket-handkerchief and buy A. M. Hunter's little book entitled: *P. T. Forsyth: Per Crucem ad Lucem*[1]. This book of Forsyth's is the greatest book in English in this century on preaching. If the members of our theological colleges had been reared on this, preaching in the Church of England would not have reached the sorry plight in which it now finds itself. Forsyth brings us back to the Bible, not in any obscurantist or fundamentalist way, but positively and with full respect for scholarship. 'If you would preach a classical gospel', he says, 'give your nights and days, your head and heart, to converse with the Bible'.[2] Forsyth insists that the Bible, properly used, becomes, by the Holy Spirit's action, the sacramental book. In the sacraments of Eucharist and Baptism the Word is visible; in true preaching it is audible. In the sacraments, the act of the cross is 'delivered to our address'—what a vivid phrase! And Forsyth can speak of the sacrament of the Word as he does of the sacrament of the Eucharist or of Baptism. Think of being an agent in delivering the act of the cross to the address of people in need of it; can there be any greater calling than that?

This leads me to touch on some very practical aspects of the art of preaching. I hope that, as I spoke those last four words, 'the art of preaching', you almost automatically registered a slight protest. How can you speak of preaching as an art? Does not this word conjure up in one's mind an element of the artificial, something of the theatrical, the putting on of a show? I admit its dangers. Preaching is far more than an art. If it be thought of

[1] SCM Press 1974.

[2] *The Gospel and Authority*, ed. M. Anderson (Minneapolis, Augsburg Publishing House, 1971), p.41.

merely as an art, it is not preaching at all. True preaching is the response to a call, to a summons. 'Whom shall I send and who will go for us?' 'Here am I; send me'. 'And he said "Go, speak . . .".' But I submit that, *in addition to this,* it is an art, and must be studied as such. There is a parallel in the use of the word 'profession' of the priesthood. Of course, the priesthood is more than a profession. The man who is to be a true priest cannot say to himself: 'Which of the following professions shall I choose: doctor, solicitor, teacher, actor, priest?'. No: there must be the response to a call; at least an element of: 'Here I stand; I can no other'. But given that, the priesthood is a profession, and calls for all the professional training and expertise and skill which can be given to its fulfilment.

Let us look, then, at those elements which need, as I believe, very careful consideration if the art of preaching is, I will not say to be perfected (for that is impossible), but to be pursued with grace and power.

I refer *first,* to the matter of simplicity of presentation. That the presentation of a message of eternal importance and of great value matters needs no elaborating. One does not present pearls wrapped in old newspaper. It is clearly possible, however, to go wrong on this matter of simplicity.

There are two kinds of simplicity. On the one hand, there is a simplicity which is the result of childishness of ideas. The preacher who is marked by *this* kind of simplicity has no depth, his range of subject and of words is small, his themes are restricted, because he has never gone far beyond the thinking which he did at theological college. It is likely that the more thoughtful members of his congregation will soon drop off, because they want to be fed on meat and are only being given milk. It is probable that the entry in Crockford's Clerical Directory of the priest we are considering will be long, for he soon exhausts what he has to say in any given place and must needs flee to some other before his nakedness be exposed. Of course, he may have recourse to clouds of seemingly learned language, with which to cover the immaturity and the confusion of his thinking. But this will hardly serve to hide him for long.

David H. C. Read, in the latest of the Lyman Beecher Lectures on preaching,[1] tells the story of a professor of theology who visited an outstation of a Christian mission in Korea and began his sermon—which had to be translated—like this: 'In our approach to ultimate reality we tend to proceed either inductively or deductively'. The translator paused, and then said, 'I am here to tell you what Jesus Christ means to me.'[2] Some people, it has been said, seem to believe that thought should be clothed in pure wool.

On the other hand, there is a simplicity which derives from profundity and is the result of good, solid, hard work. This kind of preacher has thought so hard, has read so widely, has dug so deep in the things of God and the affairs of men, has looked so searchingly into his own heart and the hearts of his fellow-men, that he is able to reduce to simple terms the treasures of Christian truth with which he has been entrusted. This kind of simplicity is hard to come by. It is not easily achieved. But it is the mark of the great teacher and preacher. It is much to be coveted.

Nor is it to be confused with 'talking down' to people. Edward Carpenter, in his estimate of William Temple in his massive book *Cantuar*,[3] makes the point that Temple

[1]*Sent from God: the Enduring Power and Mystery of Preaching* (Nashville and New York, Abingdon Press, 1974).
[2]Op. cit., pp. 106-7.
[3]Cassells 1971.

never 'talked down' to his hearers. 'To play down to an audience was utterly foreign to his nature' (p. 481). Few men of his day had thought more deeply about, nor seen more penetratingly into, the meaning of the Christian faith than had Temple. But he never insulted the intelligence of those to whom he spoke by treating them like children. People can generally detect when we do this, and they do not like it. Their *knowledge* of theology and of the things of God in general may be small. That is our opportunity to enlarge it. But we have no right to assume that their *intelligence* is small. 'Assume that your people know nothing, and keep that assumption to yourself'; the old adage may be right. But never assume that your people have no intelligence. That is a very different matter. Better, far, to preach a little above their capacity than below it. That way they will be stretched, and stretching is good for us all. *'Stand tall'*, say the physical instructors constantly. Better, far, that our people should go home saying 'I got most of what the preacher said this morning, but I could not quite follow him at such and such a point', than that they should go back unstretched, and lethargic for lack of having been challenged to 'stand tall'.

I come now, *secondly,* to the old and complex question, 'to read or not to read?'. I have no doubt at all about the answer to the question 'to write or not to write?'. The answer is undoubtedly: 'Write'. In fact, I would put it as positively as this: I doubt whether any preacher ought to go into the pulpit who has not done a good deal of steady writing at his desk by way of preparation. For writing forces the preacher to face the realities of what stares him in the face on the page before him. Does that sentence make sense? Is that paragraph logical? Does the second point emerge sensibly from the first, or would

48

it be better to invert the order? Is that the best word to express what he is trying to say, or would it be better to jettison it for another? That opening section—is it likely to grip the listeners, or will it evoke so little interest as to lead them mentally to re-invest their money or cook the dinner while he drones on? That 'finally', is it really final? And does the sermon end with a brisk final tap, or go out on a whimper?

Writing is a godly discipline. Discipline, it may be, as the writer of the Epistle to the Hebrews has it, 'is never pleasant'. Indeed, 'at the time it seems painful'. But that in the end it yields a harvest there is no shadow of doubt.

But, having written, what do you take into the pulpit? Some would say that you take a full manuscript—indeed they would be ill at ease without it. In support of this view, they could cite Phillips Brooks (author of a famous book on preaching[1] and originator of the well known and, as I think, totally inadequate definition of preaching as 'truth through personality'). He used to take a full manuscript into the pulpit and very obviously read it— and at a fast rate—to his spell-bound congregation. To which I would only reply: 'But that was Phillips Brooks!' I should regard him, rather, as the exception who proves the rule.

I believe that the reading of a manuscript or typescript from the pulpit has about it certain immense objections. It may well be that the member of the congregation who complained of his vicar's reading of the sermon: 'If he can't remember it, how does he expect us to?' was over-simplifying a complicated issue. But I see his point. The obvious presence of a manuscript to which incessant reference has to be made serves as an *intrusion* between preacher and people. That is the fundamental objection

[1]*Lectures on Preaching*, 1877.

to it. Contact, living, loving contact, between the man in the pulpit and the people in the pew is of immense importance. I must be able to look my people in the eye (I will not have the lights turned out during the sermon.). I want to see their reactions, for preaching is an essay in co-operation. How can you convey the sense of urgency, which surely must be part of your aim in preaching, if you are tied to a manuscript to which you have perforce to revert every few seconds? If you are reading an essay, or delivering an academic lecture, well and good; read your manuscript. But if you are an ambassador, pleading with men, seeking some kind of response of mind or will, that is a different matter and calls for a different approach.

If this line of argument is true, what should be taken into the pulpit? I think that a half-way course between everything and nothing is called for, except in the very rare cases of men who have such a blotting-paper kind of memory that, having done their preliminary writing work, they have no need of any reminder, as it is all in their head. I am not one of these, and I doubt whether you are. For most of us, at least an outline reminder of our written work should go with us into the pulpit, a reminder that may occupy a sheet or two of paper, which has, perhaps, the opening sentence or two in full, and the headlines, with a varying amount of 'filling-out', and a clear indication at least of the ending. This method has the advantage of keeping the preacher from wandering, of saving him from the anxiety of worrying lest he has forgotten something of importance, and at the same time of giving him that freedom from obsession with a manuscript which would stultify or limit his contact with his hearers.

At this point, I can hear an objection from some

preachers. 'I would not dare do as you suggest', they say. 'My manuscript gives me confidence.' I appreciate the point, but I would resist it. I would say to such a preacher: 'Fear not. Ask God to free you from total bondage to a manuscript. Do your preparatory work with total diligence and then, as Sunday succeeds to Sunday, take in *less*. Break away. Launch out into the deep. Trust God for confidence, and you will find a freedom which hitherto you have not known.'

Thirdly, I refer, but more briefly, to the matter of *gesture* in the pulpit. The matter is one of importance. Here again, a *via media* is called for. Not for us, at least in the respectable Church of England, flailing arms and histrionic gesticulations! But, having abjured such things, some have gone to the other extreme of using practically no gesture at all. To deprive preaching of practically all gesture by which to mark emphasis or indicate the mood of what is being said is surely to deprive preaching of an invaluable aid.

On a holiday in Norway, I attended a service and listened to a sermon which, because it was in Norwegian, I could not understand. The sermon was read apparently word for word, for the preacher had to return to look at his manuscript every few seconds. His notes-desk was high, and his hands were largely hidden. Gesture was extremely limited. Thus yet another curb was put upon the conveying of what, I hope, was a matter of supreme urgency on the heart of the preacher to the hearts and minds of his listeners.

I was interested also in the range of his voice. This was extremely limited. God had given him a voice with an extensive range, but he used only a very small part of it. If it could have been registered on one of those sensitive machines with which the radio experts face us, the needle

51

would have had very little to do. Such restriction in the range of the voice tends to encourage sleep on the part of the hearers. Why use only a fraction of what God has endowed us with? Think of an actor declaiming Shakespeare's 'To be or not to be—that is the question' and using only about three notes in which to do it. Even Shakespeare can be killed stone dead if we try hard enough.

Fourthly, I refer to the matter of *silence*.

You have probably heard the story of the preacher whose hands were enormous and whose habit it was to raise them at frequent intervals in his sermon and say 'Pause, my brethren, pause'. Perhaps he made his point in the wrong way, things being as they were! But he had a point to make.

Listen to any good actor and you will note that he draws his effect largely from the pauses which he makes. Listen to our reading of the Lessons—it is almost always too fast, too seldom interspersed with reasonable elements of silence, too hurriedly terminated with 'Here ends the Lesson', as if we can hardly wait to dash into *Te Deum* or *Magnificat*.

What is true of the reading of the Lessons is even more true of preaching. What are you trying to do as you stand in that pulpit? You are not only expounding a doctrine; you are seeking to share a vision. But if your hearers are even to glimpse that vision that you want to share with them, they must be given a chance to stop and stare. For it is a vision of something so immense that you yourself have only caught a glimpse of its outskirts.

Stopping and staring can be a re-creative experience. On a recent visit to Sweden and Norway I was impressed by the profusion of wild flowers. Some of those that delighted me most were the harebells which grew, all unasked and uncultivated, in lovely clusters by the roadside. To stop and stare at these did me more good, was more re-creative, drew out of me more of a sense of wonder, than passing hurriedly by a large bed of beautifully flowering rose-trees in my garden at home. Why was this so? The answer is that in Sweden and Norway I had time to stop and stare. At home I was too busy—in too much of a hurry.

Which things are a parable. 'The whole created universe', says Richard Holloway in his *New Vision of Glory*,[1] 'is charged with the power and grandeur of a transcendent Reality'. That is true. But all too often we are in such a hurry that we cannot stop to see it.

What is true of life in general is true also of worship. The revised services make ample provision for periods of silence, periods when we may stop and listen, stop and stare—into the Face of God. But how often the leader of the service deprives us of the opportunity to do just that.

What is true of life and of worship is true also of that particular act of worship which is preaching. If God has given us preachers something of moment to say, let us give our congregation a chance to stop and stare into that particular bit of God's truth which we have put before them. That means pauses during the sermon. It certainly means a pause at the end. How often has that gabbled ascription killed what you have sought to do in the preceding moments?

There is nothing new in all this. The Psalmist said it long ago: 'Be still and know that I am God' (46.10). But we need reminding of it. At least, I do.

I have said that in preaching we seek to share a vision with our people. We might also say that we seek to effect an introduction to a Person, the Lord Christ; an intro-

[1]Mowbrays 1974.

duction it may be for the first time, or, it may equally well be, at a deeper level. When you have introduced someone to a friend, the best thing is to stop talking and let them get to know one another, while you step back into silence. I do not need to press the analogy.

> I do not ask that crowds should throng the temple,
> That standing room be counted worth a price,
> I only ask that, as I voice the Message,
> Men may see Christ.

> I do not ask that men should sing my praises,
> Or flaming headlines spread my name abroad,
> I only pray that, as I voice the Message,
> Men may find God. . . .[1]

I would like to be a pointer.

[1]Source unknown.